For Crying Out Loud!

Over 50 Ways to Help Your Baby Stop Crying
(so you don't start)

Mary Ellen Pinkham

◀ Rub inside cover when scent fades.

Pinkham Publishing makes every effort to use acid-free
and recycled paper.

For more of our products visit www.maryellenproducts.com

PRINTED IN THE UNITED STATES OF AMERICA

Third printing: December, 2005

ISBN-13: 978-0-941298-17-9
ISBN-10: 0-941298-17-5

This book is dedicated to Andrew Pinkham, who brought so many smiles to his mother's face. I marvel at how my precious baby grew to be such a wonderful man. Though I made mistakes along the way, I did one thing right: I loved Andrew always and no matter what—and I told him so every day.
I love you, Andrew.

Mom

Babies cry. It's normal and it's natural. Newborns cry about an hour or two out of 24 and by eight weeks they're up to about three hours. (That's the peak.)

Though experts say they sometimes cry for no reason at all, crying is of course a baby's best and only way to make a request or register a complaint. Figuring out what your baby is trying to communicate can be challenging and sometimes even scary, but your efforts and your concern will bring you closer. Your baby will learn that you are there to help, and you will learn how to give the help that baby needs.

Every new mother will find some useful tips among the mom-tested suggestions that follow. Comfort your baby with them. And comfort yourself with the thought that eventually the baby will quiet down and become his or her adorable, peaceful—sleeping!—self.

*There never was a child so lovely but
his mother was glad to get him asleep.*

Ralph Waldo Emerson

SOME BASICS ABOUT CRYING

Often, after a late afternoon or evening feeding, a newborn just can't seem to get settled. The baby may awaken, pull up his knees and/or wrinkle up her face and generally seem to be having a terrible stomachache. Babies over two weeks old who continue to act like this regularly are usually called colicky. (But always check with your doctor if your baby cries persistently, just to make sure.)

There's a lot of debate about just what being colicky means, which babies actually have colic, and what to do about it. When you're faced with a crying baby, the whats and whys don't matter. The only thing that matters is figuring out a way to get the baby to stop! The most obvious causes and remedies for baby's crying come first in the following pages, and many other suggestions follow. The good news is that the worst of the crying (and colic itself) lasts only about three months.

Check the Diaper

Well, gosh, no wonder the baby's crying. Babies need a diaper change about 6-8 times a day (or 4-6 times if you're using disposable diapers).

*Diaper backward spells repaid.
Think about it.*

Marshall McLuhan

A bit of talcum/Is always walcum.

Ogden Nash

Soothe Baby's Bottom

Sometimes a baby who is teething or whose stomach
is upset has a slightly acid poop that causes little
blisters. Or she may have a rash. Pour some liquid
Mylanta into the palm of your hand and smooth
it over the affected area. Diaper rash is caused
by uric acid, and Mylanta's anti-acid formula
apparently works as well on uric acid as it does
on stomach acid. And Mylanta or its generic
equivalent is cheaper than many creams and
lotions. A little goes a long way, too.

Try a Feeding

Not sure if baby's hungry? Draw your finger across the baby's cheek. If baby turns toward the finger and opens his mouth as if to start sucking, he's probably hungry. Of course, the best way is just to offer him his usual bottle or formula and see if he drinks it.

Somebody told me I'd lose weight after the baby was born. They didn't say it was because I wouldn't have time to eat.

Gail Furgal

Having a family is like having a bowling alley installed in your brain.

Martin Mull

Offer a Pacifier

Some babies love pacifiers and find them a great comfort. As a result, their parents find pacifiers a great comfort too, and woe is you if you run out of them. Buy a few. Think of them as inexpensive insurance policies against crying. (By the way, babies can be picky about pacifiers. It's worth trying several to find one yours takes to.)

Touch Her Face

Check face, hands and feet to see if she is too warm or too hot. A too-warm baby might enjoy a lukewarm bath. (If you suspect the warmth is from fever, see page 13.) A too-cold baby needs an extra layer.

Babies are always more trouble than you thought—and more wonderful.

Charles Osgood

Mother love is the fuel that enables a normal human being to do the impossible.

Marion C. Garretty

Take Baby's Temperature

A child who is particularly fussy may be ill with an ear infection or other ailment. If your baby's temperature is elevated, or if baby is acting in a way that seems unusual, don't hesitate to consult your doctor. A good pediatrician will encourage you to call if you're concerned and will respect mom's instincts.

Burp Him

Signs baby has gas include stiffening or stretching, pulling legs up, and making a high-pitched or honking noise. (Goose mothers can ignore the last symptom.) Put him over your shoulder and gently pat or rub his back. Or lay him across your lap and pat his back.

14

If your baby is beautiful and perfect, never cries or fusses, sleeps on schedule and burps on demand, and is an angel all the time, you're the grandma.

Theresa Bloomingdale

Every baby needs a lap.

Henry Robin

Bounce Baby on Your Lap

If the usual means of burping don't work, put the baby on your lap, stomach down. Put one hand on baby's back and the other on baby's bottom, then bounce your legs gently. This may dislodge a big burp. It may also dislodge the previous meal. (Don't say we didn't warn you.) But if it helps her go to sleep, you may decide to take the risk.

Change Her Position

Maybe the baby's just feeling crampy from being in the same position for too long, so readjust her. Babies who are already upset tend to crank up the volume if they're lying on their backs. Place the baby so she is lying on her side or her stomach. (But put her on her back when she is asleep to reduce the chance of SIDS.)

*The only thing worth stealing is a kiss
from a sleeping child.*

Joe Houldsworth

Check Baby's Clothing

Is something poking or rubbing the baby (a button, zipper, a tag)? That's worth complaining about.

Children are completely egoistic; they feel their needs intensely and strive ruthlessly to satisfy them.

Sigmund Freud

The thing that impresses me most about America is the way parents obey their children.

Edward, Duke of Windsor

Strap Her On

There's no reason both baby and you should go crazy when she's fretful and you've got work to do. Slip her into an infant carrier and your hands are free to perform light work. (Postpone the phone calls, though. The person you have to call will be grateful.) And guess what? When you're not focused on the baby, you may calm down, and as a consequence, so may she.

Wrap Him Up

For nine months, a baby is used to pretty tight quarters. That's why swaddling is customary in so many cultures. Initially the baby may protest about being wrapped like a burrito, but he'll settle down. Be sure to keep his face totally uncovered. And keep swaddling snug but loose enough to allow baby's chest to move in and out as he breathes and to move his hips comfortably. Ask a friend or have the pediatrician's nurse show you how.

Give a little love to a child and you get a great deal back.

John Ruskin

You can learn many things from children. How much patience you have, for instance.

Franklin P. Jones

Change Baby's Outfit

Baby may need more or fewer layers. The best baby clothes are easy to put on and take off, like sweaters that unbutton on the shoulder, or perhaps an overall and jacket combo instead of a one-piece snowsuit.

Buckle Baby in the Swing

You've heard of a mood swing? That's a good alternative name for a baby swing. Many people find this piece of equipment is the very best solution for a crying jag. The older models had to be wound up, but the newer ones are electronic. Less work for mother.

Evolution of Mom

1st Baby:

At the first sign of distress, a whimper, a frown...you pick up the baby.

2nd Baby:

You pick the baby up when her wails threaten to wake your firstborn.

3rd Baby:

You teach your 3-year-old how to rewind the mechanical swing.

Parenting Magazine

Who is getting more pleasure from the rocking, baby or me?

Nancy Thayer

Rock On

Sit with baby in a rocking chair. If you think you'll be putting a lot of mileage on the chair, glue a strip of Velcro or grosgrain ribbon under the runners to protect the floor and keep the rocker from "traveling."

Ride the Waves

Now's the time to buy a water bed. You and baby can surf as a pair and enjoy some ocean motion.

*Looking after children is one way
of looking after yourself.*

Ian McEwain

Fix a Drink

Hold on, now: The drink is for the baby, not for
you. A colicky baby sometimes feels better after
a few sips of diluted mint or chamomile tea (tiny
bit of sugar optional) or a mix of equal parts
water and 7-Up.

We are given children to test us and make us more spiritual.

George F. Will

*H*aving a baby is like suddenly getting
the world's worst roommate, like having
Janis Joplin with a bad hangover and PMS
come to stay with you.

Anne Lamott

Try a Noisy Toy

A rattle or other noisemaker may capture the baby's attention. Or maybe the baby will just quiet down in the face of competition.

Dance Around

Put on some music that makes you happy and give baby a whirl around the room. It's okay for you to lead but not to go too fast.

No animal is so inexhaustible as an excited infant.

Amy Leslie

A baby is an inestimable blessing and a bother.

Mark Twain

Offer a Blankie

If you give baby a soft cloth diaper to hold every
time you nurse or give a bottle, with luck she'll
adopt it as a "blankie." Having something soft to
hang onto comforts many babies. A cloth diaper is
ideal because it's small, it's washable, and it's
replaceable. No matter what kind of blankie
your child adopts, get another identical one if at
all possible, just in case the original is lost or
soiled. If it's possible, launder them equally often
so they'll feel the same.

Take Him Along

Perhaps baby's cry just indicates he wants you nearby. If there's a task for which you don't want to be wearing an infant harness, bring the baby in his bassinet, or put him in one of the reclining infant carriers so he can know you're near.

*What did my fingers do before
they held him? What did
my heart do, with its love?*

Sylvia Plath

*F*amilies with babies and families
without babies are sorry for each other.

Edgar Watson Howe

Find a Quiet Place

Some babies like a lot of noise but others find it unsettling. If you're out and about, you may have trouble finding a place that's uncrowded and clean to sit down and quiet your child. Dressing or try-on rooms in clothing stores are a possibility.

Warm the Bed

Once you take your baby from the crib or cradle for midnight feedings on cool nights, putting him back into a cool bed may startle him. Place a heating pad in the empty crib until feeding is over. Remove the pad after feeding and make sure the area isn't too hot, then place baby on the warm and cozy spot.

*Babies are nature's way of showing
people what the world looks like at 2 a.m.*

Anonymous

Take a Walk

Put baby in her stroller and get going. While your 7-pound baby sleeps you can start dealing with your 75-pound weight gain and figure out where the other 68 pounds came from.

*The only thing children wear out
faster than shoes is parents.*

Jean J. Plomp

Go for a Ride

Even the fussiest babies and toddlers often drift off to sleep soon after they're gliding along the open road in a car seat.

A child is a curly, dimpled lunatic.
Ralph Waldo Emerson

Home alone with a wakeful newborn, I could shower so quickly that the mirror didn't fog and the backs of my knees stayed dry.

Marni Jackson

Tour the House

It may not be convenient or practical to go
outdoors or take a drive to nowhere. You can
comfort baby inside if you keep her in motion.
The key is to maintain an even pace. If you
have to pause, keep the stroller moving back
and forth smoothly. Don't jiggle it or jerk it
back and forth.

Wave a Fan

Babies love the soft, repetitive swoosh of a fan, and its back and forth movement can be very mesmerizing. Don't have a fan? Improvise one with a sheet of cardboard. One mom discovered the calming effect of a fan when she used a magazine to wave at and calm an infant being photographed in a studio.

*Behold the child, by Nature's
kindly law,
Pleased with a rattle,
tickled with a straw.*

Alexander Pope

Before I got married, I had six theories about bringing up children.
Now I have six children and no theories.

John Wilt

Vacuum the Floor

It's worth a shot. Many babies like the noise, and hey! At least your floor will get clean.

Buy a Fountain

If you've ever listened through a stethoscope to an expectant mother's tummy, you know that the movement of amniotic fluid sounds like ocean waves and water tumbling over rocky brooks. All these sounds induce sleep. Baby will feel right at home if you keep a decorative water fountain running in the nursery.

I don't know why they say you have a baby. The baby has you.

Gallagher

Create a Waterfall

Buckle baby into your infant carrier and bring the carrier into the bathroom. Run a bath and hope the sound of the tub filling up will lull baby to sleep. (Make sure the drain is open and stay in the room to make sure there's no flooding.) Maybe you'll have a chance to take a relaxing bath once the baby drifts off.

The only person who likes change is a wet baby!

Anonymous

Soothe and Style

Place baby in an infant seat while you work with
the blow dryer and brush. You'll tame your heir
and your hair at the same time. That steady hum
is a baby pleasure.

*The best way to make children good
is to make them happy.*

Oscar Wilde

That energy which makes a child hard
to manage is the energy which
afterward makes him a manager of life.

Henry Ward Beecher

Activate a Metronome

Tick...tick...tick...tick. That monotonous sound may be just the tick(et) to carry baby off to dreamland. And some can be timed for extended periods—up to 30 minutes.

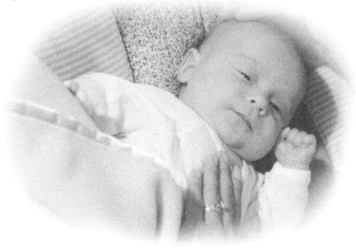

Set a Clock

The tick-tock of a clock is another soothing sound.
You can tuck one under baby's mattress. Don't
try this after your baby has seen Peter Pan.

Parents learn a lot from their children about coping with life.

Muriel Spark

Create a Mist

A running humidifier serves two purposes. Some babies find its low hum very comforting, and the moisture it adds can be helpful in too-dry rooms.

Hello babies. Welcome to Earth. It's hot in the summer and cold in the winter. It's round and wet and crowded.

Kurt Vonnegut

Never will a time come when the most marvelous recent invention is as marvelous as a newborn baby.

Carl Sandberg

Leave the Room

Take your baby out of the nursery and into the laundry or the kitchen. If you put the baby in her bassinet, stroller or carriage next to a dishwasher, clothes dryer or washing machine, the sound may remind her of the familiar territory of the womb. Desperate folk have even been known to rely on the whir of the range hood fan set at the highest speed.

If evolution really works, how come mothers have only two hands?

Milton Berle

Switch on a Fan

Not only does its slow whoosh have a calming effect, but also it moves the air around the room...Just make sure it isn't blowing directly on baby.

Wave a Scarf

Tie a light scarf or two onto the blades of the
ceiling fan. Use small ones that won't get caught
in the blades or hang down where baby can
reach them. The movement of the color may
be mesmerizing.

I wish the stork did bring babies,
preferably when they're at least
three months old.

Dale Burg

A baby is born with a need to love and never outgrows it.

Frank A. Clark

Add a Soft Spot

A good way to help all babies relax, and especially newborns, is to place a genuine lambskin under baby in the crib. (But be sure always to put baby on his back in the crib.) The soothing effect of a lambskin is universal and some call it miraculous. Many hospitals now use them in infant intensive care units. Lambskins are washable, preferably in a cold water detergent.

Take a Breath

While you're holding baby, try mindful breathing. Breathe in for three counts, hold for three counts, and breathe out for three counts. The calming effect this has on you may result in the same effect on your little one.

I have always felt that too much time was given before birth learning things like how to breathe in and out with your husband and not enough given to learning how to mother after the baby is born.

Erma Bombeck

*Infancy conforms to nobody;
all conform to it.*

Ralph Waldo Emerson

Raise the Mattress

A baby with a cold may be fussy due to a stuffed-up nose. Just as elevating your head would make you comfortable in such a situation, it will also help baby. But don't put the pillow under baby's head because of the risk of suffocation. Instead, put the pillow under the mattress itself.

Cross His Arms

Fold baby's arms across the chest and hold the baby down on the mattress gently and firmly. The gentle pressure can be soothing.

*H*ow pleasant it is to see a human countenance which cannot be insincere.

Sofia A. Hawthorne

Insomnia: A contagious disease often transmitted from babies to parents.

Shannon Fife

Offer a Heads Up

When baby is placed in the crib, put the top of her head up against the bumpers. She will feel comforted.

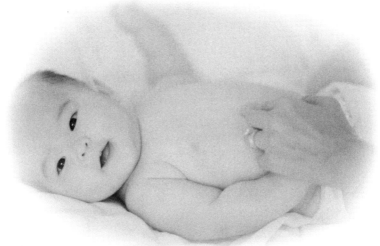

Give Him a Massage

It's never too young to get accustomed to spa
treatments. There are lots of books that tell you
how to do baby massage and there are oils
formulated specially for this purpose.

Being touched and caressed, being massaged, is food for the infant, food as necessary as minerals, vitamins, and proteins.

Frederick Leboyer

Lay Her on Dad's Chest

See if that doesn't put baby right to sleep. It's been known to have the same effect on Mom.

*There is no such thing as fun
for the whole family.*

Jerry Seinfeld

A baby is God's opinion that the world should go on.

Carl Sandberg

Read a Poem

Prop up a book or put it in a cookbook holder and read it aloud. The sing-song effect of the rhyme might please your baby. But there are babies who enjoy free verse, too.

Get a Grip

For colicky babies, the "football hold" is a must. With your elbow bent at a 90-degree hang, cup the child's head in your hand, with her face to the side. Your forearm supports the length of the child's body (stomach down), and arms and legs dangle down the side of your arms.

There are one hundred and fifty-two distinctly different ways of holding a baby—and all are right.

Heywood Broun

Change Your Moves

Another way to make baby comfortable is to hold
him as usual and try to simulate an up-and-down,
side-to-side movement that mimics the floating
sensation of being in the womb.

*O*ne touch is worth a thousand words.

Harold Bloomfield

Insanity is hereditary—you get it from your children.

Sam Levenson

Tune in the Radio

That old radio that gets only static? Don't throw
it out yet. The "white noise" is just the right sound
to put some babies to sleep.

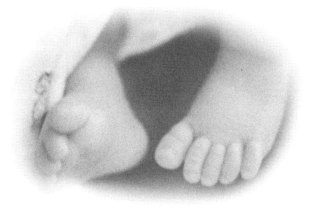

Turn on the TV

Don't use the TV as a sound machine, but if you
need a distraction of last resort, turn it on. A
fussy baby waking up in the middle of the night
may nod off after watching the Late (or Late
Late) Show or infomercials. The only danger is
that you might start ordering vegetable slicers
in your middle-of-the-night stupor.

Between the dark and the daylight when the night is beginning to lower comes a pause in the day's occupations. That is known as the children's hour.

Henry Wadsworth Longfellow

Try a Dip

Maybe it's a reminder of what the amniotic fluid feels like, but more than one mother claims that the greatest way she found to calm a fretful baby is to dip baby's feet in warm water for a minute. If that doesn't do the trick, maybe it's time for a calming double dip. You and baby could slip into a warm bath together.

Perhaps parents would enjoy their children more if they stopped to realize that a film of childhood can never be run through for a second showing.

Evelyn Nown

101

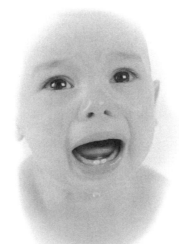

People who say they sleep like a baby usually don't have one.

Leo J. Burke

Keep It Simple

When you hold or rock a colicky infant, face a blank white wall or window shade. This helps reduce the visual stimulation to which colicky babies are overly sensitive.

Add Some Spring

If you put springs or spring casters on the crib
legs, you can rock the baby in the crib.

It is no small thing that they, who are so fresh from God, love us.

Charles Dickens

We find delight in the beauty and happiness of children that makes the heart too big for the body.

Ralph Waldo Emerson

Go to the Tape

Tape the sounds of rushing water, your dishwasher, your dryer or the vacuum cleaner, and leave the tape machine near the crib. A flick of the switch and you've got soothing noise right at hand.

Buy a Sound Machine

Try playing ocean waves, birds singing, a gentle rain shower or the sounds of a thunderstorm. So what if your little one's favorite is a thunderstorm? Maybe he'll grow up to be a lawyer.

Every child comes with the message that God is not yet discouraged of man.

Rabindronath Tagore

A babe in a house is a well-spring of pleasure.

Martin Tupper

Sing a Song

To your baby, of course you're Madonna—even the one who sings. Take advantage of this wonderful period when baby is the most devoted fan you may ever have. To add a little fun to the experience, sing solos to a karaoke CD.

Turn on the Music

Tony Bennett...Raffi...Bach? Influence your tyke's taste and play something you enjoy. Music, which soothes the savage beast, should have the same effect on a baby. You might even get into a mellow mood yourself.

Perhaps a child who is fussed over gets a feeling of destiny; he thinks he is in the world for something important and it gives him drive and confidence.

Benjamin Spock, M.D.

Babies are a nice way to start people.

Don Herold

Crank up the Music Box

Find one that plays a lullaby. A music box will also make a wonderful keepsake when baby becomes a grownup. If you have more than one, start a collection. (Of music boxes, not of children.)

Wait a Bit

Some infants just routinely cry for five minutes or so before falling to sleep. However, if the crying persists, offer your baby help.

Never fear spoiling children by making them too happy. Happiness is the atmosphere in which all good affections grow.

Joe Houldsworth

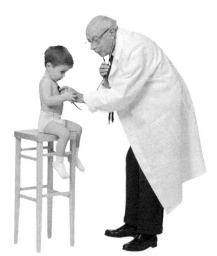

Rule Out Allergies

If your child has frequent distressful bouts of
crying, ask your pediatrician if milk or formula
allergies should be ruled out.

A sweet child is the sweetest thing in nature.

Charles Lamb

To see helpless infancy stretching out her
hands, and pouring out her cries
in testimony of dependence, without
any powers to alarm jealousy,
or any guilt to alienate affection,
must surely awaken tenderness in
every human mind.

Samuel Johnson

Hand Baby Over

When you've struggled with a bawling baby for too long you may be on the verge of tears yourself, so accept help from anyone who offers. What's more, being held by someone else may startle the baby into silence.

A Final Thought

Touch, hold, and cuddle your baby. Gaze into her eyes. Tell him how much he is loved. Babies understand lots more than we know. The knowledge you are there to help will eventually help baby be at peace. Though you might also want to invest in some earplugs.

The End

What Worked for You?

I love baby tips! Send me one of your all-time favorites. If I use it in any of our publications or books, I'll send you a free book. In the event of duplication (and I'm sure there will be be many), the book will go to the person whose hint I open first.

I'm looking forward to hearing from you.

Mary Ellen

Send your tips to:

Pinkham Publishing
Box 10
Grand Rapids, MN 55744

Or e-mail me at:

m.ellen@bitstream.net

A Time to Remember...

On the following pages, capture your own precious
memories and tips you use with your baby.

My Best Memories & Tips

_____

_____

_____

_____

_____

_____

_____

_____

_____

My Best Memories & Tips

_____

_____

_____

_____

_____

_____

_____

_____

_____

My Best Memories & Tips

_____

_____

_____

_____

_____

_____

_____

_____

_____

My Best Memories & Tips

_____

_____

_____

_____

_____

_____

_____

_____

_____

My Best Memories & Tips

_____

_____

_____

_____

_____

_____

_____

_____

_____

_____

My Best Memories & Tips

_____

_____

_____

_____

_____

_____

_____

_____

_____

My Best Memories & Tips

_____

_____

_____

_____

_____

_____

_____

_____

_____

BYE-BYE BABY STAINS

"After the miracle of child birth comes the miracle of laundry."

How does one little baby generate such a mess? So many moms asked me for a way to remove formula, spit-ups and other baby stains that we decided there was a need for a one-of-a-kind product. Squirt it on and watch the most impossible stains disappear...even old stains from hand-me-downs will be "all gone."

Two formulas: Formula 1 for whites and colorfast items, and Formula 2 for colored clothing. Each 8 oz. bottle is only $4.99, plus $1.50 per bottle for shipping and handling.

Go to www.maryellenproducts.com

LOOKING FOR MORE GREAT GIFT BOOKS?

Check out our web site. We offer discount prices and we'll even pay for the mailing or shipping.